Dedications

To my husband, Jeff, and children, Nekisha, Nikki, and Seth. Thank you for always supporting me.

Note from the Author

Rita Thomas

"If I rise on the wings of the dawn, if I settle on the far side of the sea, even there your hand will guide me, right your hand will hold me fast." (Psalm 139:9-10, NIV)

God holds our hands in every situation and place in our lives. From our birth until now, God has always been present, holding our hand. Even as we sleep, he holds our hand and stirs us to waking moments.

This book is a journey into your life and relationship with God. Take it personally and be ready to grow your relationship with God by affirming your trust and belief in Him.

CONTENT

Introduction
Part 1 Who I Am Affirmations

I Am More Than Enough
I Am Confident in Who I Am
Everything I Need is Already Mine
My Heart is Opened
I Want It All

Part 2 What I Believe About God
God is Goodness
God is a Provider
God Never Changes
God is Compassionate
God is Everything I Need

Part 3- As a Christian, I Declare and Affirm
I Have a Gift
I Recognize God's Presence
I Wait on God
I Must Work It
I Rule Over My Thoughts
I Am Not Afraid
I Walk Forward
I Forgive
I Will Not Die in the Wilderness
I Honor God

I Am Blessed
I Am Healed
I Am Protected
I Am Loved
I Prosper in Storms
I Expect Miracles
I Am Known by God
I Rest
I Am Grateful
I Am Powerful
I Release It
I Believe
I Am Free of Overthinking
I Can Make It
I Walk by Faith
I Listen to Hear
I Talk Through It
I Am Chosen
I Have a Destiny
I Trust God

Afterward

Introduction

Why Should We Affirm for Forty Days?

Affirmations are essential for our spiritual growth as they help us focus on God instead of the situation. They are rooted in scripture to empower us, and our hope in redemption through Jesus and the resurrection is the substance of our faith. The number forty is significant in the Bible as it is mentioned over 146 times as a period of testing and trials, highlighting the relationship between faith and hope. Our expectations of God's power enable faith to work, and when we trust Him, He makes our expectations a reality, and we witness the evidence produced.

As we progress in our spiritual journey, we should always remember that God has chosen us and will always be with us, guiding us through every step. The forty days that Jesus spent appearing after His resurrection is a powerful reminder of the true strength of faith in action. Our daily affirmations help us recognize and honor His presence, power, and divine will for our lives. By humbly surrendering our need for control and placing our trust in His guidance, we can rest assured that our future path will be clear and prosperous.

So, let us continue to affirm His presence, power, and purpose daily and build our faith through the Word of God.

Affirmation One: *I Am More Than Enough*

I am more than enough. I am confident in my abilities and know I have what it takes to achieve my goals. Genesis 1:27 reminds me that God made man and woman in his image. Not only did He make me in His image, but He blessed me and gave me dominion over every circumstance.

How do I know that I am enough? I know this because He predestined every moment of my life. God saw me in my unformed state and knit me together in my mother's womb. He breathed life into me, and I became his living creation.

I am my father's child and heir to his throne. I will not be measured by others because there is no one like me. So today, I declare and affirm that I am enough.

Dear Father,

Thank you for your guidance and support in helping me realize I can achieve my destiny. Your unwavering love and encouragement have given me the strength and confidence to pursue my dreams. Amen.

Affirmation Two: *I Am Confident in Who I Am*

WHAT I BELIEVE AND AFFIRM

I belong to God, and His thoughts about me are the only things that matter. I affirm that I am His and confident in who I am. In 1 Corinthians 6, I am reminded that I belong to God and was bought with a price.

Why should I be confident? I am His child, redeemed and chosen with a purpose. Wherever I go, I am always in His presence. I am confident that evil cannot diminish my spiritual purpose because God's truth guides me through life. I am a conqueror with Him as my guide.

So today, I declare that I am confident in who I am because I know who I belong to.

MY PRAYER

Dear Father,

Everything that I am is because of your presence. Whether I am standing on the highest mountain or down in the deepest valley, you are always by my side. Through every challenge and every triumph, you have been there to hold my hand and guide me toward success. Thank you for teaching me to love myself. Amen.

Affirmation Three: *Everything I Need is Already Mine*

I believe that God has gone before me and given me everything I need to succeed. It's up to me to recognize and utilize the resources available to achieve these goals. I know this because, in Deuteronomy 31, Moses bid farewell to the Children of Israel. As he left, he assured them that God would go before them and possess the land for them, destroying all who opposed them.

But when does God go before me? It is said that even as I developed in my mother's womb, God created a unique purpose and plan for my life. And when I accepted salvation, I received His spirit, which guides me daily towards His plan for me. My success is deeply connected to His purpose and the path He has created for me. So, all I have to do is believe and receive it.

Dear Father,

Thank you for leading the way, standing by my side, and shielding me from harm. I reaffirm my faith in you and everything you have given me. In Jesus name, Amen.

Affirmation Four: *My Heart is Opened*

I believe that God has opened the eyes of my heart so that I may be enlightened with purpose, filled with riches, inheritance, and great power. It is stated in Ephesians 1 that the same power that raised Christ from the dead is present within me now as a believer. With this Spirit, I am unstoppable and powerful beyond measure.

Why is it important that the eyes of my heart are opened? I am reminded that I was chosen for a purpose before the creation of the earth, predestined for God's will and pleasure. I have been adopted as an heir through Jesus Christ, and it is important for me to keep my heart open to receive all that God has planned for me.

So today, I affirm that my heart is open, and I am ready to use the powers that God has given me as His child.

Dear Father,

Thank you for the desire to seek your will and purpose for my life. Please guide me in using my spiritual gifts to serve you and others. In Jesus name, Amen.

Affirmation Five: *I Want It All*

I believe that God desires to prosper me, but first, I must learn to obey His will. I affirm that my prosperity is a product of my faith, and obedience is what puts it in motion. I know this because, in Job 36:11, I learned that obeying and serving God will lead me to spend the rest of my life in prosperity and contentment.

But how is obedience connected to my faith and the Will of God? Obedience is more than just following rules - it demonstrates my trust and love for God. Without action, faith is meaningless. By following God's will, I draw closer to Him and show gratitude for all He has done for me. This obedience also brings blessings and prosperity into my life.

So today, I declare my faith and commitment to obey your will for my life. I trust you know what is best for me, and I want it all. I want to prosper in every area.

Dear Father,

Thank you for guiding me to obey and prosper according to your will. I want it all. Amen.

Affirmation Six: *God is Goodness*

I believe that God's goodness is evident in everything that He does. He rejoices over me every day. I know this because Psalm 145, 8-10 says that the Lord is gracious and merciful. He is patient with me, and his love is reliable and indestructible.

How do I know that God is goodness? I know this because God's goodness is not dependent on the circumstance. Regardless of what is happening, God never changes. He is always good. When I fix my eyes on Him, I am comforted by His constant love and care. He has proven His goodness to me time and time again throughout my life. He never wavered in His love for me. And even when I didn't and couldn't love myself, He loved me unconditionally.

So today, I reaffirm that God is goodness and His love is all around me in everything I do.

Dear Father,

Thank you for your goodness. It is your grace and love that keep me every day. In Jesus name, Amen.

Affirmation Seven: *God is a Provider*

I believe that God is a provider, my Jehovah-Jireh. There is nothing that I need or want that God will not provide. I know this because in Genesis 22, God provided Abraham a ram in the thicket, and He will provide for me.

How does God provide? God provides me with all the necessary resources for my survival, but that's not all. The Holy Spirit watches over my heart and mind, leading me on the right path to grow closer to God's love and guidance. Through obedience, He provides spiritual gifts that increase prosperity in every area of my life. If I withhold nothing from God, He will withhold nothing from me. He is my provider; my faith opens heaven's windows so I may live in prosperity and contentment.

So, today, I recognized that God is my source and provider.

Dear Father,

Thank you for my gifts. Teach me how to make the most of them to bring glory to your name. Amen.

Affirmation Eight: *God Never Changes*

I believe that God is the same yesterday, today, and tomorrow; His love never changes. I know this because Malachi 3:6 is a powerful reminder that God is unchanging and constant. In times of uncertainty and chaos, I can find comfort in knowing that God's love never changes, and His mercy never fails.

How do I know that God never changes? His character and promises remain steadfast no matter what happens in my life. I can always trust His love, mercy, and grace, even during difficult times. God's unchanging nature gives me hope and peace, knowing He is always with me and will never leave or forsake me.

So, I declare that God is the same yesterday, today, and forever, and His love will never change.

Dear Father,

Thank you for never changing. No matter what is going on in my life, your unwavering presence and steadfast love give me the strength and courage to face any challenge. Amen.

Affirmation Nine: *God is Compassionate*

I believe that God is caring, and His compassion is not limited. He offers it to each of us. I know this because Psalm 145:8-9 says that God is kind and compassionate. Even when I am difficult to love because of my disobedience, He is patient and slow to anger.

How do I know that God is compassionate? He found me when I was lost. God lifted me up and placed me in His presence when I was down. He covered and cleansed me of my sins. He taught me the meaning of love and how to extend it to myself and others.

Today, I am reminded that God is always with me, no matter where I am, and that He is overflowing with love and compassion.

MY PRAYER

Dear Father,

Thank you for your tender mercies that keep me going today, for every good and perfect gift you give, and for protecting me from danger, seen and unseen. Thank you for blessing me, my family, and those around me. In Jesus name, Amen.

Affirmation Ten: *God is Everything I Need*

I believe that God is all I need to be successful and safe in this world. I affirm that my trust is in God and Him alone. I know this because, in Genesis 15:1, God tells Abram not to fear but to trust in Him because He will be his reward. As with Abram, I know that when I put my faith in God, He will be my shield and protection against harm. That is His promise; He is everything I need to succeed and prosper.

Why is God all I need to be successful? God knows my past, present, and future and has a path planned for me. If I stay focused on God rather than the situation, God will lead me through difficult times, around pitfalls, and into a bright and prosperous future. So, I declare that God is everything I need and trust in Him.

Dear Father,

You are my all and everything. As I focus on you today, give me the knowledge and wisdom to make the right decision and be a blessing to someone else. I know you are everything I need, and I trust you completely. Thank you for always being there for me. Amen.

Affirmation Eleven: *I Have a Gift*

I believe that I have been blessed with a unique gift from God. I know this because 1 Peter 4:10-11 highlights the different spiritual gifts God bestows upon us to accomplish His will and bring glory to His name. I am confident that my gifts are part of His divine plan for me and are good and perfect in every way.

How do I know that my gifts are from God? I am certain that my gifts are from God because He revealed them to me through the Holy Spirit, and they continue to grow within me daily. I am committed to using my gift to its full potential and pursuing my calling passionately and purposefully. With the help of the Holy Spirit, I will grow and develop my gift daily, and I will use it to honor God and fulfill His will for my life.

Dear Father,

Thank you for giving me the gift of love, for your love snatched us from darkness into light. Through Jesus, I am redeemed and made whole in your goodness. I will forever be grateful and thankful for your compassion and love. Amen.

Affirmation Twelve: *I Recognize God's Presence*

I believe that God's presence lives inside me, and when I recognize it and make room for it, I am empowered to possess all that God has given me. I know this because, in 1 Corinthian 3, we are told that our bodies are God's temple and His spirit dwells within.

But how does God's Spirit live in me? As a believer, God's Spirit acts as a conduit of power to develop my connection to Him to grow my spiritual gifts. The amount of power I receive depends on my willingness to recognize His presence and give room to His purpose. No room, No power! His presence guides me in truth, empowers me, and ensures my future. So today, I affirm your presence in every aspect of my life. If anything is in your way, move it because I want everything you want and desire for me.

Dear Father,

I invite you to be a part of every aspect of my life. I have no secrets from you; every door is open for your presence. I belong to you, and when you are with me, I am home. Amen.

Affirmation Thirteen: *I Will Wait on God*

I believe that the battles I face are not mine alone and that I must wait for God to guide me on the right path to victory. I know this because Lamentation 3:25 tells me that if I have hope in God and seek him first, He will see that I am protected from all harm.

So, what does it mean to wait on God? It means seeking His protection and growing closer to Him as I expect an answer. It also means trusting in His plan and being patient even when I don't know the outcome. So, while waiting may be difficult, I can find peace knowing that His solution is always better than mine

So today, I affirm that I will wait on you, God, as you direct me in the next steps in my life.

Dear Father,

For me, waiting is hard. I know you have all the answers, and everything happens for a reason, but sometimes, you are silent when I ask you questions or have concerns. But I trust that this waiting is all a part of your plan for my life. In Jesus name, Amen.

Affirmation Fourteen: *I Must Work It*

I believe that God has given me gifts to use for his glory, but it will not work unless I work it. I affirm that my gifts are God-given and unique, and I must work to bring them forth. As mentioned in 1 Corinthians 12, we are given gifts according to the Spirit. Therefore, I was given these gifts so that I may live a life that is pleasing to Him, bearing fruit in every good work.

How do I work my gifts? To effectively use the gifts that God has given me, I must deepen my understanding of God. Through the guidance of the Holy Spirit, I can learn how to use these gifts to make a positive impact on my life and the lives of others. The key is to stay open and obedient to God's will. When I align with His plan, my gifts will pave the way for blessings of prosperity and success. So, I affirm that I will listen and obey your will so that I may develop my gifts for your glory.

MY PRAYER

Dear Father,

May my spirit be obedient that I may hear and obey. I never want to rebel against you but be aligned with your will. In Jesus name, Amen.

Affirmation Fifteen: *I Rule over My Thoughts*

I believe that what I think is as important as what I do to be successful. I affirm that my thoughts are fixed on God and not a situation because I rule over my thoughts. I know this because Colossians 3 tells me to set my mind on the things above. Setting my mind on God changes my focus.

Why is it important to change my focus? It is not a matter of if things will happen but when. Focusing on God gives Him room to fight my battles and change my situations. You see, it is only when I focus on God that I see Him in the middle of my situation or circumstance, moving and rearranging things to work out for my good.

So today, I affirm that God is my focus, and my thoughts are aligned with him.

Dear Father,

My heart belongs to you. I depend on you for my success. May your blessings enrich my soul and draw me closer to you. Thank you for your love and grace. In Jesus name, Amen

Affirmation Sixteen: *I Am Not Afraid*

I believe that fear is not of God; therefore, I am not afraid, for God will be with me wherever I go. In Joshua 1:9, God commands me to be strong and courageous, to keep his laws in my heart and on my lips so that I may prosper and be successful.

Moreover, I have learned from John 14:27 that my heart should be filled with peace, not fear. And to remind me of his promise, God has sent me the Holy Spirit, who teaches me to walk in faith and not fear.

I understand that fear can prevent me from receiving God's promise and prospering in God. Fear is my adversary, and I have equipped myself with the shield of faith to conquer it. So, I declare that I am not afraid, and fear has no hold over my life.

Dear Father,

Your guidance and support give me the confidence to tackle any obstacle. I trust you completely to lead me on the right path. Thank you for being there for me always. Amen.

Affirmation Seventeen: *I Walk Forward*

I believe my life is in front of me. So, I walk forward and not backward in my past. I know this because Isaiah 43:18-19 assures me that God is doing something new in me. He is carving a path through the wilderness and a river in the desert so I can leave my past behind and focus on what lies ahead.

It is important for me to keep my eyes in front because my past does not limit God's plan for my life. He has a unique purpose for my life; I embrace it with open arms. I refuse to allow my past mistakes and failures to hold me back. Instead, I look ahead with hope and confidence that God's plan for my life is unfolding. He is my guide and protector, and I trust Him completely. So, I choose to walk forward in faith, knowing that my future is secure in His hands, and I am excited to see what He has in store for me.

Dear Father,

Your love redeems and restores me through your Word. I am now free from my past and embracing a new life filled with hope, faith, and prosperity. Amen.

Affirmation Eighteen: *I Forgive*

I believe that forgiveness is a powerful tool against the enemy. When my heart is filled with unforgiveness, I can't be trusted with the power and prosperity of God. So, when I forgive, God opens doors of freedom so that I may receive His blessings. According to Matthew 6:14-15, I must forgive others, just as God has forgiven me.

My success is tied to forgiveness, and it is what God expects of me. If I don't forgive, God will not forgive me or extend grace towards me.

Through forgiveness, I not only release the person who has hurt me, but I also release myself from the burden of anger and bitterness. It's important to note that there is no limit to the number of times I must forgive, for God has no limit on the number of times He forgives me. So today, I forgive because God forgave me.

Dear Father,

Thank you for forgiving me and giving me the wisdom to set others free. I am grateful for your grace. Amen.

Affirmation Nineteen: *I Will Not Die in the Wilderness*

I believe it is a sin not to take advantage of the blessings that God has given me. In the Book of Numbers. it says that the Children of Israel perished in the wilderness because they were rebellious and refused to take what God had given them. I will not suffer the same fate and die in the wilderness.

But what exactly is the wilderness? It is a place of familiarity and comfort. However, it is not the land that God has intended for me. The things that await me are exceedingly good, and if I trust Him, He will ensure that I enter that Promised Land. Therefore, I am unafraid of the unknown and accept what God has given me.

Today, I choose to move away from my comfort zone and declare I will not die in the wilderness.

Dear Father,

Thank you for the Promised Land that lies before me. I am determined to defeat every giant and obstacle in my path. I refuse to perish in the wilderness, so I am moving towards the new land and promises. Amen.

Affirmation Twenty: *I Honor God*

As a Christian, I believe that I must honor God in all aspects of my life. In Proverb 3:9 it states that I should give God my best and first offerings to honor Him.

So, how do I honor God? It is through my attitude, affection, and actions. As a Christian, I strive to do my best in everything because that is what God expects of me. I always keep a positive attitude and demeanor, knowing I represent my Father, God. As a sign of my affection towards Him, I give God a tenth of my first earnings and abilities as my tithe. When I honor God with excellence, even in the smallest things, He blesses me with His wisdom, knowledge, and prosperity.

Today, I declare that every action I take, every decision I make, and every word I speak will be done with excellence. I do so to honor and show gratitude to the one who made me, loves me, and cares for me.

Dear Father,

Through every gift, you teach me what excellence looks like, and I am grateful for your guidance. Amen.

Affirmation Twenty-One: *I Am Blessed*

I am blessed beyond measure. I am blessed, my family is blessed, and my situation is blessed. I believe that the blessings I receive come from God, who has graciously opened the storehouse of heaven and showered me with abundant prosperity. I am blessed whether in the city or the country, at home or at work. I know this to be true because Deuteronomy 28 promises that I will be blessed above all others if I obey God. I am confident that many blessings await me if I remain faithful to Him.

How do I know that I am blessed? I have received His blessings as a promise through inheritance. People look at me, and they fear me because the mark of God is upon me; I am God's chosen one, and He will always be there to guide and protect me. So, today, my blessings are chasing and overtaking me so that I may prosper in God's Will.

Dear Father,

Thank you for blessing me with your wisdom and grace. I honor you today through obedience and bless your name. In Jesus name, Amen.

Affirmation Twenty-Two: *I Am Healed*

I am completely healed in every aspect of my being - emotionally, mentally, physically, and spiritually - because of my connection with God. I know this because, in Jeremiah 30:17, God promises to restore my health and heal my wounds.

What does it mean to be healed and restored? It means to walk in wholeness. I cannot be healed if I am not whole, and healing can only come through Jesus Christ. He did not die to send me to Heaven, but to bring Heaven to me in healing and restoration of my heart. From my heart, I am healed, restored, and redeemed to wholeness through His love, not through my own actions. Jesus is my redeemer because he restored me back to God.

So, today, I walk in healing because I am restored through the blood covenant of Christ.

Dear Father,

I walk in healing because you restored me through the blood of Jesus. Thank you for your endless love and compassion toward me. In Jesus name, Amen.

Affirmation Twenty-Three: *I Am Protected*

God protects me in all areas of my life. Under His protection, nothing can separate me from His love. According to Isaiah 54:17, no weapon formed against me shall prosper, and any tongue that rises against me shall be judged.

So, how does God protect me? He keeps me safe from both seen and unseen dangers that may threaten me. Even when I'm going through tough times, I know that God is always with me, guiding me through the fire and flames of life. God wants me to trust and believe. He knows what's best for me and will always be my protector.

So today, I rest in the knowledge that God protects me in all things.

Dear Father,

You are my protector, my guide, and my friend. I trust in your plan for my life, and I pray that you continue to walk with me every step of the way. In Jesus' name, I pray. Amen.

Affirmation Twenty-Four: *I Am Loved*

I am loved by myself and God. My belief in this truth is rooted in the powerful words of Isaiah 43, which remind me that I am precious in God's eyes, honored, and loved beyond measure. I am filled with comfort and security, knowing that I am not alone in this world. Wherever I go and whatever I may face, He is with me, guiding and protecting me.

Why am I worthy of love? I am worthy of love because I am created in God's image, and His Spirit lives within me. God's perfect love for me is evident in His sending His son, Jesus, to guide me back to Him. This selfless act of love is a testament to God's boundless grace and mercy. As I journey through life, I find strength and comfort in knowing that I am loved and cherished by myself and my Heavenly Father. This unwavering love empowers me to face challenges with courage and determination.

Dear Father,

Your love is evident and present in every area of my life. I am thankful for your love and compassion. Amen.

Affirmation Twenty-Five: *I Prosper in Storms*

I believe storms are perfect for me to open my wings and fly above the clouds. Life is full of storms, and they are inevitable. However, how I respond to them is rooted in what I believe. James 1:3-4 says that storms test my faith, and they make me perfect and complete, lacking in nothing. So, instead of running from the storms, I embrace them and let them shape me into a better version of myself.

Why do I prosper in the storm? As I soar above the clouds, I am reminded that there is beauty in the storm. The rain may pour down, the thunder may roar, and the winds may howl, but I am a conqueror, and nothing that comes against me shall prosper. I prosper because I believe, have faith, and trust God to protect me. So, I welcome the storms today, for they will strengthen me as I prosper and grow.

Dear Father,

I remain steadfast in my belief. I know that trials come to test me, but I will not waver in my faith. I am stronger than any storm because You live in me. Amen.

Affirmation Twenty-Six: *I Expect Miracles*

Every morning, I wake up expecting God's miracles in my life. God has promised me a land that belongs to me, and until I receive it, I believe that miracles will occur when I seek God's presence in my life. My belief is supported by Job 5:8-9, which states that if I present my requests to God, He will perform wonders beyond measure. Therefore, I expect miracles that only God can achieve, regardless of the situation.

Why do I have such expectations? It is because God loves me and cares for me. Every morning that I wake up is a blessing from my Father. When I lay down at night, it is a blessing that He has carried me all day. I am precious in God's eyes; He is my God and Father, and I am His child. As a Christian, I have a covenant with God, a promise, and I don't resist His love but welcome it with open arms. So, today, I expect my Father to provide me with miracles that only He can do.

Dear Father,

You are the source of my life, my comfort and joy. Thank you for every miracle that you give daily. Amen.

Affirmation Twenty-Seven: *I Am Known by God*

God knows me by name and cares about every detail of my life. He knows who I am from the depth of my heart because He lives in me. He understands my thoughts and feelings and knows what is best for me. I know this because Isaiah 43 tells me that God knows me personally and has redeemed me. He summoned me by name, and I belong to Him.

How does God know me? He knows me because He made me for His glory and anointed me with his purpose. He knows my voice when I call because I have a relationship with Him. I am not just a number or a statistic to Him but His beloved child, made in His image.

So, today, I am grateful to know that God knows me by name and that I can always call on him.

Dear Father,

You know me. I am known to you and by you as your child. I am thankful that you care for me. Amen.

Affirmation Twenty-Eight: *I Rest*

The Lord is my shepherd and guide, and I rest in his presence. He leads me into green pastures and calm waters where I can rest and feel safe. Even during chaos and turmoil, God prepares a place for me that is secure and free from harm. He desires that I have peace and rest in His arms. This is evident in Psalm 23, where it says that God leads me beside still waters and makes me lie down in green pastures, providing a place of peace and prosperity.

Why am I at rest? Because I know that God is with me every step of the way. Even when I face danger and threats, I am not afraid because God walks with me. He anoints my head with His glory and makes me prosper in the presence of my enemies. Like a sheep, I hear my Master's voice and follow. No matter what I need, God has it and will give it to me. So today, I rest in the presence of the Lord.

Dear Father,

Rest is important and I am thankful that I found it safe in your arms. Amen.

Affirmation Twenty-Nine: *I Am Grateful*

As I wake up each morning, I am grateful for all the good things in my life. I know it was not a coincidence that I woke up in my right mind this morning, but rather a part of God's plan. Each day, I am blessed with another opportunity to serve Him and fulfill my purpose.

As I go throughout the day, I am reminded of the words of 1 Thessalonians 5:16-18, which urge me to always rejoice, pray, and give thanks to God in all circumstances. No matter what is going on in my life, whether good or bad, it will all work out for my good. So today, I want to give thanks for your blessings and live each day with a grateful heart.

Dear Father,

I am grateful for every gift of your love to me. I don't know why you love me, but I am grateful that you do. Amen.

Affirmation Thirty: *I Am Powerful*

I believe in the power of God and His presence within me. This power resides inside me, and I accept it wholeheartedly. I am not ashamed and make room for what it has for me. In Luke 17:21, Jesus says I have been given the power to achieve the good I desire because God's Kingdom dwells within me.

So, how do I know that I am powerful? In Acts 1:8, it states that I have received the power of the Holy Spirit, and this power is manifested in me. As my relationship with God grows, this power also increases. It acts as a shield of protection from the enemy's fiery arrows. I can move mountains, change situations, and defeat the enemy through it. No matter what comes my way today, I can change or defeat it through God's power that lives in me.

Dear Father,

You once told me that I could move mountains if I had faith as small as a mustard seed. So today, I command it to move and get out of my way because I believe in You. Amen.

Affirmation Thirty-One: *I Release It*

Today, I am letting go of everything that hinders me from reaching my full potential. I have faith in God, and I put my trust in Him. He is the one constant in my life, and I will no longer conform to what others believe about me. I have wasted too much time on that. In Proverbs 4:25-27, I am instructed to keep my eyes on God and follow the path He has directed for me. I understand that every situation and person in my life has a season, and when that season is over, I must let it go. My future is not my past, so I release it all today and walk in God's plan for my life.

Why should I release it? God will not operate in a life that is filled with clutter. Removing those things that are detrimental to my success allows God to take root and operate in my life. There is nothing that He won't do for me if I choose to walk with Him and release everything holding me back. The choice is always mine, and I choose to release it daily.

Dear Father,

It's difficult for me to let go of the people and things that have been a part of my life, but I trust you. Amen.

Affirmation Thirty-Two: *I Believe*

WHAT I BELIEVE AND AFFIRM

I believe in God, and I am fully committed to Him. I believe that Jesus is the Son of God and that through my faith in Him, I am saved and will live with Him eternally. This belief is based on John 3:16, which states that God loved me so much that He gave His only Son so that I may have eternal life and not perish.

Why should I believe it? God could have left me in sin, but He promised never to leave or forsake me. So, He gave Jesus, His very best so I could return to Him. I know that God always has a plan for everything He does, and nothing is wasted, so I know my life has a purpose.

WHAT I BELIEVE AND AFFIRM

Dear Father,

I believe that I am precious to you, and I know you always want what is best for me. Thank you for your love and the gift of salvation. Amen.

Affirmation Thirty-Three: *I Am Free of Overthinking*

I am learning to embrace a new mindset of freedom by letting go of overthinking. God knows what is best for me and that every situation will work for my good. The words of Psalm 94:19 is a constant reminder that God is always by my side, comforting and bringing joy in every circumstance. By turning to prayer and releasing my worries and fears, I can find peace and joy. I trust in God's goodness and wisdom and no longer feel the need to question why things happen.

As I focus on God and deepen my relationship with Him, I can hear His voice more clearly and receive His encouragement and direction. With God as my guide, I am free from the burden of overthinking and can live a positive, fulfilling life. I trust that God has a plan for me and that everything that happens is a part of that plan.

Dear Father,

Please guide me in your truth; teach me your ways. I want to become more like you. Amen.

Affirmation Thirty-Four: *I Can Make It*

WHAT I BELIEVE AND AFFIRM

I can make it and overcome any obstacle that comes my way. With the wisdom and strength of my faith, I am fully equipped to handle whatever the day brings. As Philippians 4:12-13 reminds me, I can find contentment in any situation because I can do all things through Christ who strengthens me.

Life is unpredictable and challenging, but I know I am not alone. The Holy Spirit is always with me, offering guidance, comfort, and wisdom and empowering me with the strength to face any challenge. So, when trials come, I am not shaken. I stand firm in my faith, drawing upon the strength of Christ within me, for I am confident that I can make it through anything that comes my way.

MY PRAYER

Dear Father,

Your presence gives me the strength to overcome obstacles, and your wisdom helps me make good decisions amid chaos. Thank you for your guidance, in Jesus' name. Amen.

Affirmation Thirty-Five: *I Walk by Faith*

I have learned to walk by faith instead of sight. It is an essential part of my journey as a believer. Even when I am lost and unsure where to go next, I know I can trust God to guide me. 2 Corinthians 5:7 reminds me that I must walk by faith, not sight. This verse means I must trust God and believe in His plan for my life.

What is walking by faith? It means surrendering control and allowing God to work in my life. It means trusting He has a purpose, even when I can't see it. This is not always easy, but I have found that the more I let go and trust God, the more peace and joy I experience. Therefore, I affirm that wherever you lead me, I will follow because I trust you to know what is next in my life.

Dear Father,

I embrace the unknown and keep moving forward, confident in your love and guidance. I trust that you will walk beside me every step of the way. Thank you, in Jesus' name. Amen.

Affirmation Thirty-Six: *I Listen to Hear*

WHAT I BELIEVE AND AFFIRM

I listen for understanding- not just with my ears but also with my heart. When I listen with my heart, I open myself up to be led by the Holy Spirit, who provides clear instructions and guidance. In Proverbs 4:20-21, I am encouraged to turn my ears toward the Word of God, to listen and obey His commands.

Why do I need to listen? In a world full of distractions and noise, it's easy to find myself overwhelmed and needing clarification. If I am not careful, I will miss the instructions and directions that I need to move forward in my journey. That's why calling out to God and listening for His response is so important. When I do, I can be sure that He will answer. No matter what happens today, I will find time to be still and listen because God knows my path and will give me good directions.

WHAT I BELIEVE AND AFFIRM

Dear Father,

No matter how busy my day may get, I will never be too preoccupied for you. I enjoy our time together. Amen.

Affirmation Thirty-Seven: *I Talk About It*

I talk to God, my Father, about every aspect of my life. I believe that when I meet God in my secret place, He listens and is pleased. According to Hebrews 4:16, I can approach God's throne of grace confidently and receive mercy and grace in times of need. In those moments of prayer and reflection, I find comfort and strength in knowing that He cares for me.

Why should I talk to God? Talking to God is important because He loves me and wants to be a part of my daily life. When I am happy, He rejoices with me. When I am sad, He comforts and guides me on the right path. If I am faithful and ask for anything in prayer, trusting that I will receive it, my Father will not withhold it from me. I know my Father cares for me and always listens; therefore, I can always talk to Him.

Dear Father

I find it easy to talk to you about anything. Even when I haven't made the best decisions, you guide me to make the right decisions. I am glad I can talk to you. Amen.

Affirmation Thirty-Eight: *I Am Chosen*

I believe God chose me before the world's creation and made me holy and blameless in his sight, as it says in Ephesians 1:4. I am without blame because God sent Jesus to take that blame away from me. As a believer, I am humbled by the fact that He knew and loved me even before I was born. That is an example of real love, and it gives me the strength to know that I have a purpose.

So, how do I know that I am chosen? In John 15:16, Jesus assures me that it was not me who chose Him, but rather, He chose me. Despite my flaws and imperfections, He chose me, broken and lost, to spread His love throughout the world. Because of His love, He blesses and multiplies my fruit, transforming me from a barren vessel to a fruitful one overflowing with spiritual abundance. I don't know why He loves me, but I'm glad He does.

WHAT I BELIEVE AND AFFIRM

Dear Father,

Thank you for choosing me and prospering me in every area. Today, I pray that I will show the same love that you give to me. Amen.

Affirmation Thirty-Nine: *I Have a Destiny*

I have a destiny that only God can fulfill. I know that God is shifting and moving things around for a reason. Nothing happens without a purpose in my life. As in 1 Corinthians 2:9 it says, eyes have not seen, nor ears heard, nor can I imagine what God has prepared for me because I love Him. I may not be able to comprehend God's plans for me, but I know that they are good and will lead me to my destiny.

So, how do I know that I have a destiny? I was once a broken vessel, lost and wandering in the darkness, but God found and restored me, giving me a new purpose and hope. His plans are still a mystery, but I trust He knows what is best for me. I believe that my destiny belongs to God and Him alone and that He will guide me every step of the way.

MY PRAYER

Dear Father,

I have a destiny that only you control. My life belongs to you. Wherever you send me, I will go. My life is in your hands. Amen.

Affirmation Forty: *I Trust God*

WHAT I BELIEVE AND AFFIRM

In every situation and moment in my life, I trust God. There have been times when I didn't know how or when I would make it through, but God showed me the way. He always finds a way out of nowhere. In 1 Corinthians 2:9, I learned that if I stop trying to understand everything and lean into God by trusting Him, He will make my path straight and lead me on the right path.

So why do I trust God? I trust God because He is faithful and never fails. No matter what happens, He prevails. In pain, I trust Him to comfort me and give me strength. In affliction, I trust Him to heal me and restore me. In loneliness, I trust Him to be my companion and friend. In persecution and rejection, I trust Him to defend and lift me. In everything, He makes it work together for my good, and that's why I trust God.

MY PRAYER

Dear Father,

I trust in you in every situation and moment, knowing that you will never leave or forsake me. Even when all else fails, I believe that you are still there. I will continue to trust in you all the days of my life. Amen.

AFTERWORDS

I hope these affirmations will help you strengthen your relationship with God, our loving Father. As you may already know, our words and beliefs hold immense power. Therefore, I encourage you to make it a habit to talk to God every day. He is always there to listen, comfort, and guide you through life's ups and downs.

By affirming your faith in God, you can tap into His infinite wisdom and power. You can experience His love and grace in your life, and you can find the strength, courage, and wisdom to face any challenge that comes your way. So, I invite you to repeat these affirmations every day and see how they transform your life:

Remember, God is always with you and will never leave or forsake you. He wants you to experience His love and grace in your life and guide you toward righteousness. So, I pray that God will bless you and your family. May He grant you the strength, wisdom, and courage to face any challenge that comes your way. May He fill your heart with His love and grace and guide you toward righteousness.

www.ingramcontent.com/pod-product-compliance
Lightning Source LLC
Chambersburg PA
CBHW071253130726
47998CB00003B/1179